JAMES BOND 007™
COLLECTION FOR GUITAR

MP3

The included DVD-ROM contains sound-alike and play-along MP3s of each song. To access these recordings, insert the DVD-ROM into a computer, double-click on My Computer, right-click on the disc icon, and select Explore. (Mac users can simply double-click the disc icon that appears on the desktop.) The MP3s are located in the "**MP3s**" folder.

TNT² CUSTOM MIX

In addition to the MP3s, the DVD-ROM contains our exclusive TNT 2 software that you can use to alter the audio mixes for practice, loop playback, and change keys and tempos.

For installation, follow the instructions at left to explore the disc, and double-click on the installer file. Installation may take up to 15 minutes.

System Requirements

Windows
7, Vista, XP
1.8 GHz processor or faster
1.3 GB hard drive space, 2 GB RAM minimum
Speakers or headphones
Internet access required for updates

Macintosh
OS 10.4 and higher (Intel only)
1.3 GB hard drive space, 2 GB RAM minimum
Speakers or headphones
Internet access required for updates

Produced by
Alfred Music Publishing Co., Inc.
P.O. Box 10003
Van Nuys, CA 91410-0003
alfred.com

Printed in USA.

ISBN-10: 0-7390-9456-4 (Book & DVD-ROM)
ISBN-13: 978-0-7390-9456-3 (Book & DVD-ROM)

Clifford Essex Paragon De Luxe guitar photo: Madeline Newquist
Recordings by Artemis Music Limited, except all guitars, "Live and Let Die," and "Nobody Does It Better" by Leaky Spigot

Dear Reader,

On the back cover of this book you will find a photograph of my Clifford Essex Paragon De Luxe guitar, which has played a significant part in my career as a professional musician and in establishing a musical identity for the James Bond films.

On June 21, 1962, I recorded the "James Bond Theme" in CTS Studios in London, England, with an orchestra led by John Barry.

Because of the work that John Barry and I had done on earlier films, the editor of *Dr. No*, the first James Bond film, asked John Barry to adapt and arrange a melody supplied by Monty Norman and record it in the same exciting and forceful style. With my guitar, fitted with a DeArmond pickup played through a Vox 15-watt amplifier, I provided the exact sound that complemented John Barry's arrangement—an arrangement and recording that became the flag waver for the James Bond series of films.

In this book you will find wonderful transcriptions and guitar tablature of some of the best James Bond songs, plus a DVD-ROM with play-along tracks and software to help you perfect your performance.

I know you will enjoy this book as much as I have.

—Vic Flick
VicFlick.com

The book *Vic Flick Guitarman* is available at Amazon.com.

Contents

*See the instructions on pg. 1 to access the MP3s and TNT 2 player. The software will allow you to fine-tune the instrument mix (especially useful for songs with two guitars) and access other special features for practice.

DIAMONDS ARE FOREVER

Music by JOHN BARRY
Lyric by DON BLACK

Verse 1 lyrics:

Dia-monds are for-ev - er,_____ they are all I need to please me,_____ they can stim - u - late and tease me,_____ they won't

Cont. in slashes

Diamonds Are Forever - 3 - 1

FOR YOUR EYES ONLY

Music by BILL CONTI
Lyrics by MICHAEL LEESON

For Your Eyes Only - 3 - 1

FROM RUSSIA WITH LOVE

Words and Music by
LIONEL BART

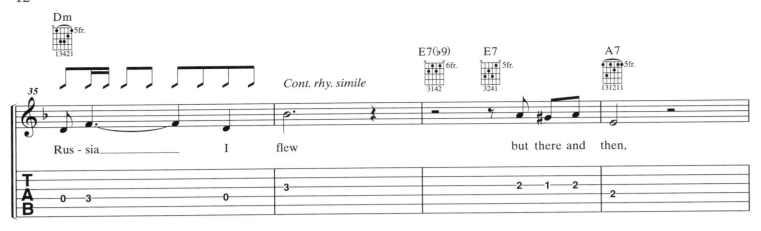

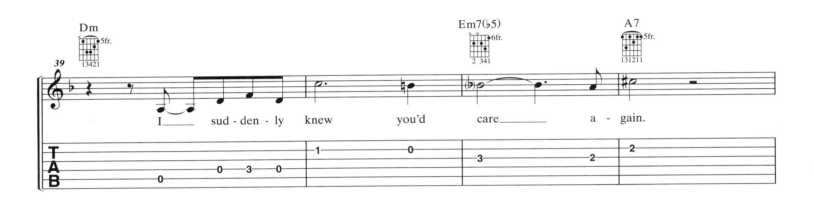

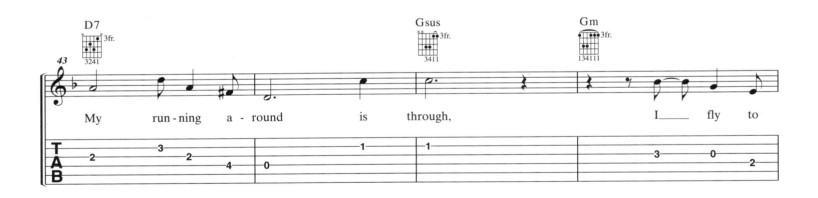

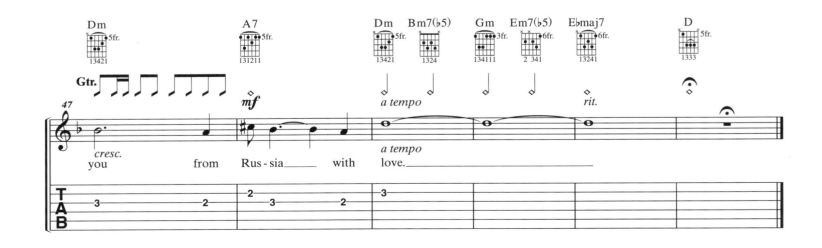

GOLDFINGER

Moderately ♩ = 103

Intro:

Music by JOHN BARRY
Lyrics by LESLIE BRICUSSE
and ANTHONY NEWLEY

Verse 1:

Gold - fin - ger,   he's the man,   the man with the Mi - das touch,   a spi - der's touch.   Such a

Goldfinger - 3 - 1

LIVE AND LET DIE

Words and Music by
PAUL McCARTNEY and
LINDA McCARTNEY

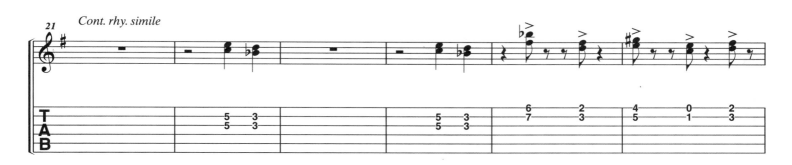

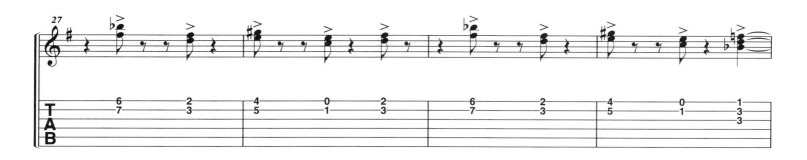

Bridge:
w/reggae feel

What does it mat - ter to ya, when you got a job to do,__ you got - ta

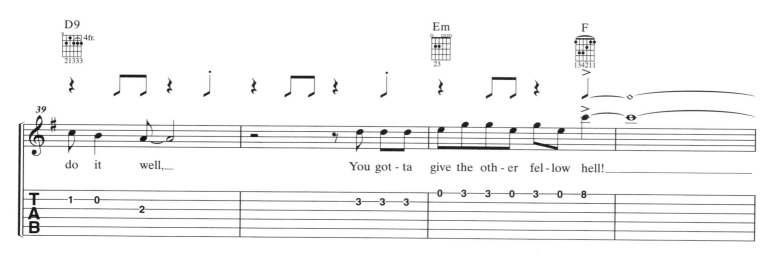

do it well,__ You got - ta give the oth - er fel - low hell!__

Interlude:

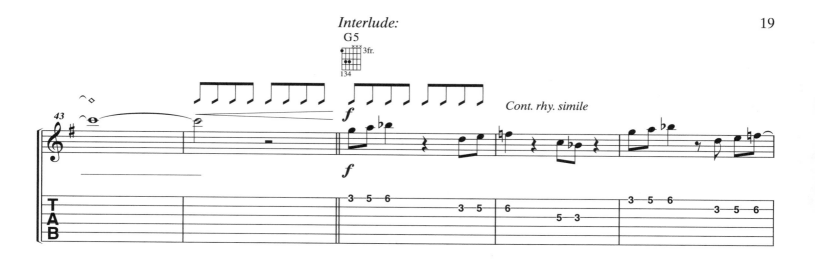

D.C. al Coda

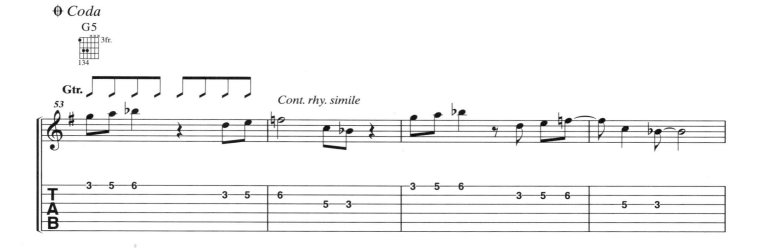

Live and Let Die - 4 - 4

JAMES BOND THEME

from *Dr. No*

By MONTY NORMAN

James Bond Theme - 3 - 1

With a slight swing feel

On Her Majesty's Secret Service - 5 - 4

THUNDERBALL

Music by JOHN BARRY
Lyrics by DON BLACK

*To match record key, Capo I

Moderately ♩ = 92

*Recording sounds a half step higher than written.

Verses 1 & 2:

1. He al - ways runs while oth - ers walk. He
2. He knows the mean - ing of suc - cess. His

acts while oth - er men just talk.___ He looks at this
needs are more so he gives less.___ They call him the

world and wants it all, so he strikes like
win - ner who takes all, and he strikes like

Thunderball - 3 - 1

TOMORROW NEVER DIES

Moderately ♩. = 74

Words and Music by
SHERYL CROW and MITCHELL FROOM

Tomorrow Never Dies - 6 - 1

38

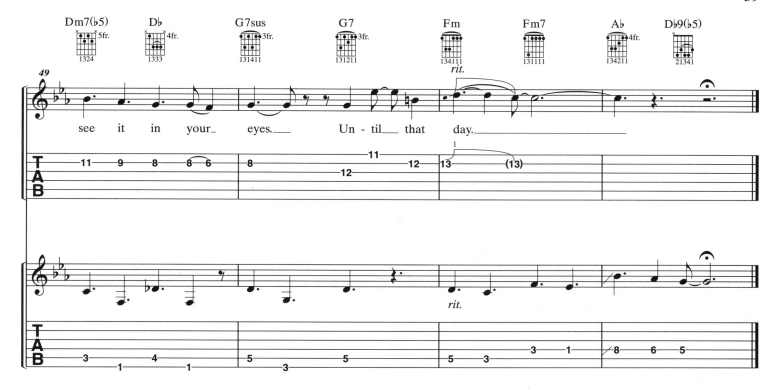

see it in your eyes. Un - til that day.

Verse 2:
Darling, you've won; it's no fun,
Martinis, girls and guns.
It's murder on our love affair,
But you bet your life, every night
While you're chasing the morning light,
You're not the only spy out there.
It's so deadly, my dear,
The power of wanting you near.
(To Chorus:)

A VIEW TO A KILL

Words and Music by
JOHN BARRY and DURAN DURAN

A View to a Kill - 4 - 1

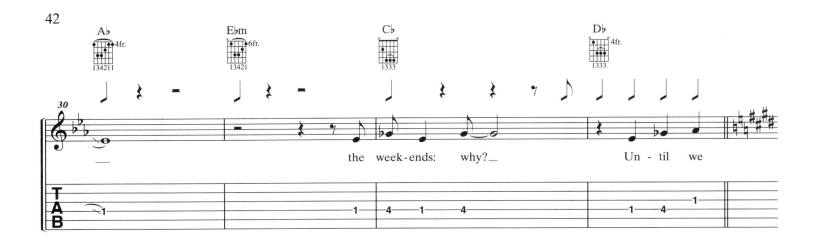

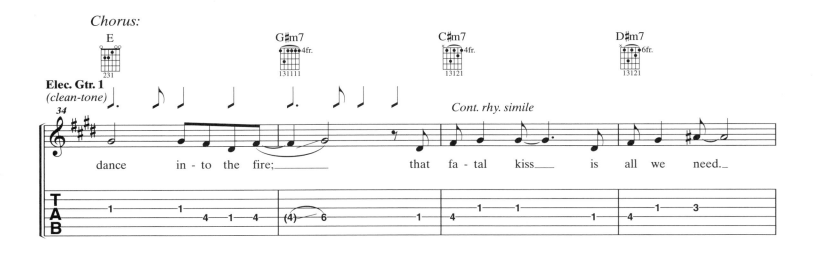

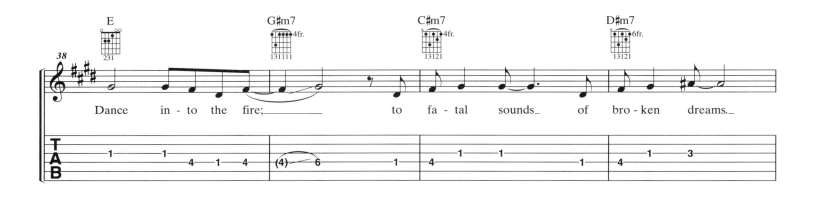

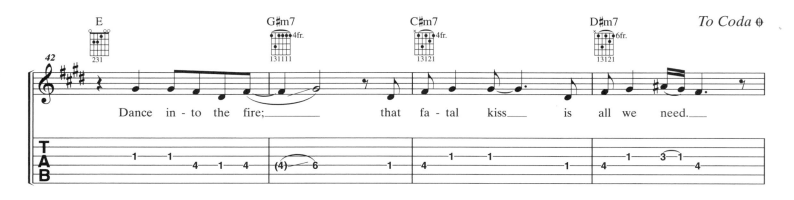

Verse 2:
Choice for you is a view to a kill.
Between the shades, assassination standing still.
The first crystal tears fall as snowflakes on your body.
First time in years, to drench your skin with lovers' rosy stain.
A chance to find a phoenix for the flame,
A chance to die, but can we…
(To Chorus:)

YOU ONLY LIVE TWICE

Music by JOHN BARRY
Lyrics by LESLIE BRICUSSE

You Only Live Twice - 3 - 1

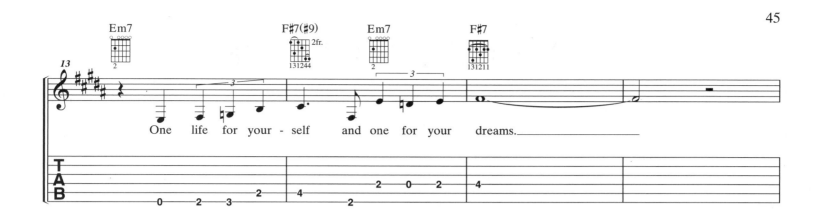

One life for your-self and one for your dreams._____

w/Rhy. Fig. 1 (*Elec. Gtr.*)

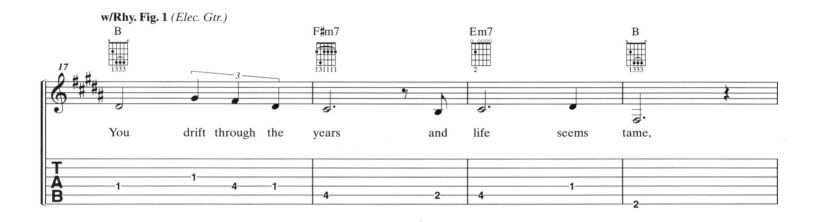

You drift through the years and life seems tame,

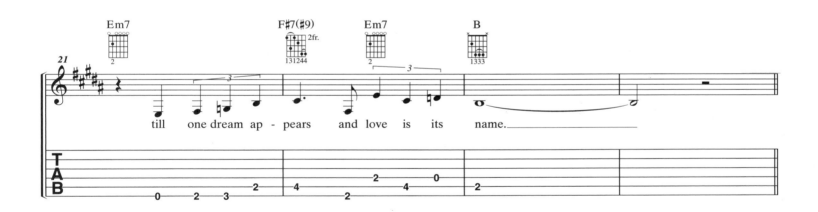

till one dream ap - pears and love is its name._____

Bridge:

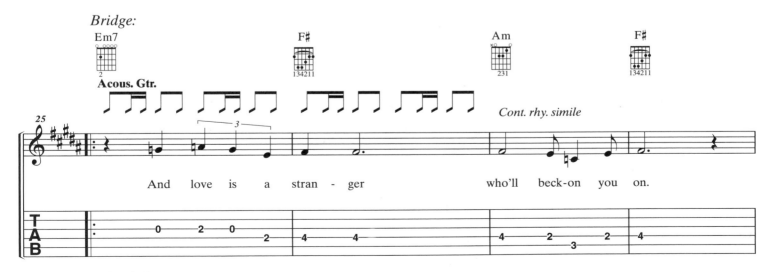

And love is a stran - ger who'll beck-on you on.

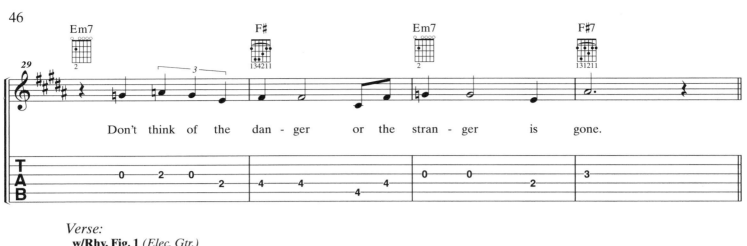

Don't think of the dan - ger or the stran - ger is gone.

Verse:
w/Rhy. Fig. 1 *(Elec. Gtr.)*

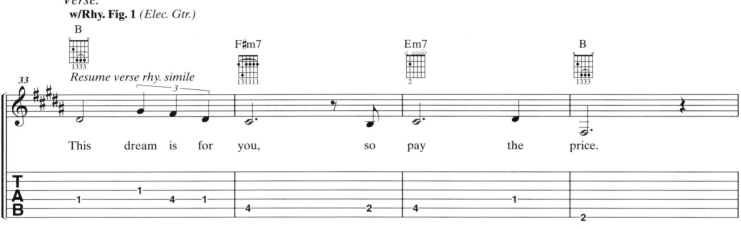

Resume verse rhy. simile

This dream is for you, so pay the price.

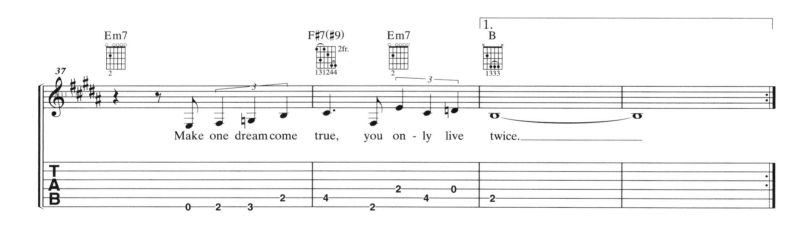

Make one dream come true, you on - ly live twice._____

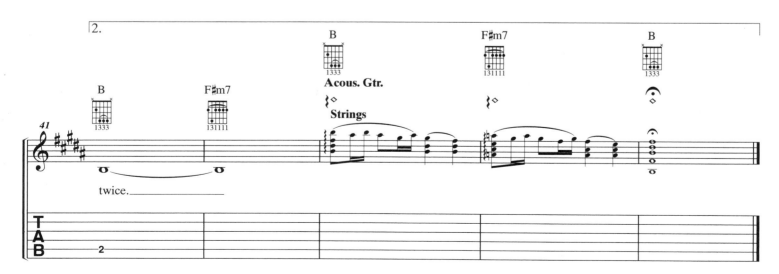

twice._____

TABLATURE EXPLANATION
TAB illustrates the six strings of the guitar.
Notes and chords are indicated by the placement of fret numbers on each string.

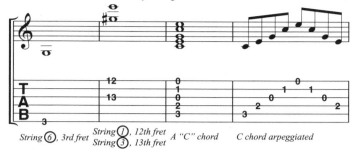

String ⑥, 3rd fret   String ①, 12th fret   A "C" chord   C chord arpeggiated
String ③, 13th fret

BENDING NOTES

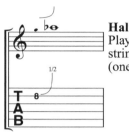

Half Step:
Play the note and bend
string one half step
(one fret).

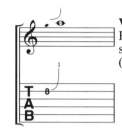

Whole Step:
Play the note and bend
string one whole step
(two frets).

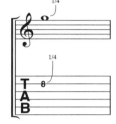

Slight Bend/
Quarter-Tone Bend:
Play the note and bend
string sharp.

Prebend (Ghost Bend):
Bend to the specified
note before the string is
plucked.

Prebend and
Release:
Play the already-bent
string, then immediately
drop it down to the
fretted note.

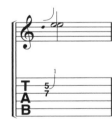

Unison Bends:
Play both notes and
immediately bend the
lower note to the same
pitch as the higher note.

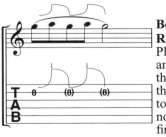

Bend and
Release:
Play the note
and bend to
the next pitch,
then release
to the original
note. Only the
first note is
attacked.

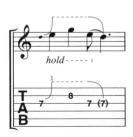

Bends Involving
More Than One
String:
Play the note and
bend the string
while playing an
additional note
on another string.
Upon release, re-
lieve the pressure from the additional note
allowing the original note to sound alone.

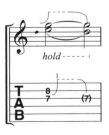

Bends Involving
Stationary Notes:
Play both notes and
immediately bend the
lower note up to pitch.
Return as indicated.

ARTICULATIONS

Hammer On:
Play the lower note, then "hammer" your finger to the higher note. Only the first note is plucked.

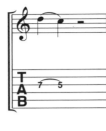

Pull Off:
Play the higher note with your first finger already in position on the lower note. Pull your finger off the first note with a strong downward motion that plucks the string—sounding the lower note.

Legato Slide:
Play the first note and, keeping pressure applied on the string, slide up to the second note. The diagonal line shows that it is a slide and not a hammer-on or a pull-off.

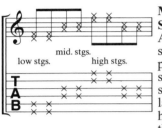

Muted Strings:
A percussive sound is produced by striking the strings while laying the fret hand across them.

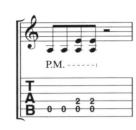

Palm Mute:
The notes are muted (muffled) by placing the palm of the pick hand lightly on the strings, just in front of the bridge.

HARMONICS

Natural Harmonic:
A finger of the fret hand lightly touches the string at the note indicated in the TAB and is plucked by the pick producing a bell-like sound called a harmonic.

RHYTHM SLASHES

Strum Marks/ Rhythm Slashes:
Strum with the indicated rhythm pattern. Strum marks can be located above the staff or within the staff.

Single Notes with Rhythm Slashes:
Sometimes single notes are incorporated into a strum pattern. The circled number below is the string and the fret number is above.

Artificial Harmonic:
Fret the note at the first TAB number, lightly touch the string at the fret indicated in parens (usually 12 frets higher than the fretted note), then pluck the string with an available finger or your pick.

TREMOLO BAR

Specified Interval:
The pitch of a note or chord is lowered to the specified interval and then return as indicated. The action of the tremolo bar is graphically represented by the peaks and valleys of the diagram.

Unspecified Interval:
The pitch of a note or chord is lowered, usually very dramatically, until the pitch of the string becomes indeterminate.

PICK DIRECTION

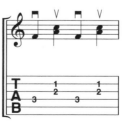

Downstrokes and Upstrokes:
The downstroke is indicated with this symbol (⊓) and the upstroke is indicated with this (V).